It's Time to Celebrate

# DAY OF THE DEAD

Written by
Rebecca Phillips-Bartlett

KidHaven
PUBLISHING

Published in 2026 by
KidHaven Publishing, an Imprint of
Greenhaven Publishing, LLC
2544 Clinton St., Buffalo, NY 14224



**Written by:** Rebecca Phillips-Bartlett
**Edited by:** Noah Leatherland
**Designed by:** Ker Ker Lee



**Cataloging-in-Publication Data**
Names: Phillips-Bartlett, Rebecca.
Title: Day of the Dead / Rebecca Phillips-Bartlett.
Description: Buffalo, NY : Kidhaven Publishing, 2026. | Series: Its time to celebrate | Includes index and glossary
Identifiers: ISBN 9781534550032 (pbk) | ISBN 9781534550049 (library bound) | ISBN 9781534550056 (ebook)
Subjects: LCSH: All Souls Day--Juvenile Literature | Day of the Dead—Juvenile Literature | Holidays—Juvenile Literature
Classification: LCC GT4995.A4 P45 2026 | DDC 394.266 --dc25



Manufactured in the United States of America

CPSIA compliance information: Batch #CSKH26
For further information contact Greenhaven Publishing LLC at 1-844-317-7404.

Please visit our website, www.greenhavenpublishing.com.
For a free color catalog of all our high-quality books, call toll free 1-844-317-7404 or fax 1-844-317-7405.

Find us on

**Photo Credits** – Images are courtesy of Shutterstock.com. With thanks to Getty Images, Thinkstock Photo, and iStockphoto.

Recurring images – KanKhem, Edge Creative, Vector Tradition, Justin Mark. Cover – KanKhem, Edge Creative, Vector Tradition, Justin Mark. 2–3 – Tatiana Gordievskaia. 4–5 – Fer Gregory, Yuganov Konstantin. 6–7 – Lemberg Vector studio, BNP Design Studio, Vector Tradition. 8–9 – Carlos Ivan Palacios, ProStockStudio. 10–11 – Anna Klepatckaya, Timski. 12–13 – Arlette Lopez, AGCuesta, Studio_G. 14–15 – Arina P Habich, Arina P Habich. 16–17 – AGCuesta, Diego Grandi, Quetzalcoatl1. 18–19 – Yuganov Konstantin, Bisams. 20–21 – Lucy.Brown, Lecker Studio. 22–23 – Kobby Dagan, Yuganov Konstantin.

# Contents



Words that look like <u>this</u> can be found in the glossary on page 24.

# It's the Day of the Dead!

Hi! I am Felipe. I am dressed up because I am celebrating Día de los Muertos. Día de los Muertos means Day of the Dead. The Day of the Dead is a Mexican festival.

The Day of the Dead is celebrated in parts of the United States too.

The Day of the Dead lasts from the 31st of October to the 2nd of November. The name might sound sad, but it is an important celebration. It is about remembering and celebrating our ancestors.

# The Day of the Dead Story

The story of the Day of the Dead starts over 2,000 years ago with a group of people called the Aztecs. The Aztecs often offered food and tools to people who had died. These things were believed to help people reach the afterlife.

In around 1500 CE, a Christian festival called All Souls' Day was brought to the Americas. This day was about remembering people who had died.

Aztec traditions around death and All Souls' Day traditions blended together to create the Day of the Dead.

# Celebrating the Day of the Dead

On the Day of the Dead, it is believed that the border between the living world and the spirit world disappears. People get to celebrate with their loved ones who have died.

Families make displays called ofrendas to welcome their loved ones.

Lots of skull and skeleton decorations are put out during Day of the Dead. This reminds people that death is part of life. The skeletons are often doing silly things, which makes them less scary.

# Craft Corner

## Let's Make a Silly Skeleton

**You will need:**

- Cotton swabs
- Black paper
- White paper
- Scissors
- Glue
- Colored pencils

Scissors are sharp. Always have a grown-up with you while using scissors.

**How to make a silly skeleton:**

1. On your black paper, lay the cotton swabs out to look like a skeleton. Use the picture as a guide!

2. Glue your cotton swabs to the black paper.
3. Cut a skull shape out of the white paper.
4. Glue the skull to the black paper.
5. Use colored pencils to decorate.

How will you decorate the skull? You could use lots of bright colors!

# Making the Ofrenda

The ofrenda is one of the most important parts of the Day of the Dead. Families make ofrendas to leave offerings for their loved ones who have died. Ofrendas help them find their way to their family.

Ofrendas have photos of the people who are being invited to visit. They also contain things the people liked, such as their favorite foods. Most ofrendas are decorated with candles and flowers called marigolds.

# Cooking Corner

## Let's Make Sugar Skull Cookies

Sugar skull cookies make a yummy treat for your ofrenda.

**You will need:**

- 1/2 cup (100 g) of sugar
- 1/2 cup (100 g) of butter
- 1 teaspoon (5 mL) of vanilla extract
- 2 eggs
- 2 1/2 cups (300 g) of plain flour
- 1/4 cup (30 g) of cornstarch
- Colorful icing

## How to make sugar skull cookies:

1. Heat the oven to 390 degrees Fahrenheit (200 degrees Celsius).
2. Mix the sugar and butter together.
3. Mix in the eggs and vanilla.
4. Mix in the flour and cornstarch.
5. Roll out the dough to around 0.2 inch (0.5 cm) thick.
6. Use a cookie cutter to cut the cookies out. Bake for up to 10 minutes.
7. Once cool, decorate your cookies with icing so they look like skulls.

# On the Day of the Dead

To prepare for our ancestors, we make the ofrenda. Making the ofrenda reminds us to think about our loved ones and remember the things they liked. I love hearing stories about my ancestors.

On the Day of the Dead, there is also a huge parade. For the parade, lots of people dress up as skeletons or wear makeup or masks to make them look like a skull.

# Creative Corner

## Let's Design a Skull Mask

Get ready to celebrate the Day of the Dead by designing your own skull mask. You could even stick your drawing on cardstock and cut it out to make a real mask.

**You will need:**

- Some paper
- Colored pens or pencils

**How to design a colorful skull mask:**

1. Draw a face shape on your paper. It should be around the size of your head.
2. Draw eye holes.
3. Decorate your mask with bright colors and flowers.

# Day of the Dead Around the World

While the Day of the Dead started in Mexico, it is celebrated in many countries around the world. Different countries have their own ways of celebrating.

In Guatemala, people fly huge kites to remember their ancestors on the 1st of November.

In Bolivia, a type of bread called t'anta wawa is made for ofrendas. T'anta wawas are loaves of bread shaped as babies. Each year, there is a competition to see who makes the largest bread baby.

# It's Time to Celebrate the Day of the Dead

Now you know all about the Day of the Dead. You also have lots of ideas about how people celebrate around the world. So, it is time to celebrate the Day of the Dead!

How will you celebrate the Day of the Dead?

Perhaps you will dress up in bright clothes and paint your face to look like a skull? Maybe you will take some time to think about your family's history. There are many ways to celebrate!

# Glossary

| | |
|---|---|
| **afterlife** | in some religions, the place people go after death |
| **ancestors** | people in a family who lived a long time ago |
| **Aztecs** | a group of Indigenous people who lived in Mexico a long time ago |
| **festival** | a time when people come together to celebrate a special event |
| **spirit** | a being that is not part of this world, such as a ghost |
| **traditions** | beliefs and actions that are passed down between people over time |

# Index